D1335194

COMHAIRLE CHONTAE ÁTHA CLIATH THEAS
SOUTH DUBLIN COUNTY LIBRARIES

CASTLETYMON BRANCH LIBRARY
TO RENEW ANY ITEM TEL: 452 4888
OR ONLINE AT www.southdublinlibraries.ie

Items should be returned on or before the last date below. Fines,
as displayed in the Library, will be charged on overdue items.

John McAuliffe

NEXT DOOR

(signature)

Gallery Books

Next Door
is first published
simultaneously in paperback
and in a clothbound edition
on 2 July 2007.

The Gallery Press
Loughcrew
Oldcastle
County Meath
Ireland

www.gallerypress.com

ISBN 978 1 85235 425 1 *paperback*
       978 1 85235 426 8 *clothbound*

A CIP catalogue record for this book
is available from the British Library.

Contents

for Nancy

A Pyramid Scheme

An old Cortina's come to rest
at the end of the road. The weeks pelt
its glass and steel, invisibly
emptying it and making free

with some random person
who strips the interior and then,
accompanied, helps himself
to tyres, battery, driveshaft, exhaust.

The bodywork flakes and scabs.
Going nowhere, looking naked, mad,
mirrorless and windowless,
it gathers accessories

like one of those disused roadside crannies:
plastic bags, a seatful of empties
and, adjacent, a holed mattress, a pallet,
a small fridge — the whole lot useless, inside out,

till the rusting shell starts half-stories,
the kind that make it first notorious,
for the children who will have to learn
what goes on at night, or could go on,

then a shelter for their elders,
a try-out zone, its vacant doorless
frame a guarded hiding place, its fag-end
still paying a dividend.

Context

The traffic's non-existent,
the sun is first blocked out,
then difficult,

in my face, a loud glare
when I turn the corner
up the private road to where

I'll spend an hour
with one or other daughter
of the rich, reading Chaucer

or Congreve or Shakespeare
while the day prepares
to disappear,

casting into shadow the pool,
the garden's converted stable
and ancestral stele,

too near to it this evening
for anything
but mute approving

glances down the hill
where the beautiful
suburbs climb and sprawl

while the girl copies out:
'"There's vice that most
I do abhor" — Relate

quotations to the title,
to the *social* as well
as to the personal.'

The Graveyard

The trees
in their ivy ballgowns
state the obvious,

but the irregular stones
upright or at an angle
are unimprovable:

they gesture and whisper
about seeing no future
in peace or rest.

The formal lawn
is so even
it's almost not there.

Painted a glossy black,
the ornate gate
creaks and shines.

Moving In

Her garden, once a selling point, is a state already.
Its furthest, dampest end is conifers, debris
and constant dark. And it's a zoo of noise,
sucking road and sky into the old semi's acoustic shadow.
There used to be one long bed of cultivated earth,
planted with care and effort,
where she — the last owner-occupier —
matched each half-season to a different colour

so that one unknown variety ceded ground
to another unheralded
profusion of whites or reds or blues,
much as her post continues
to arrive, credit card and book club promotions
giving way to seasonal round robins
bearing good news, best wishes and written postscripts
from the colonies' retiring outposts.

Now I hardly step or look outdoors,
riveted by the school and fiscal years'
eternal returns, but unable to ignore
how one good neighbour or another
declares with careless, proprietary accent,
'She loved that garden', as I half-plan
uprooting even the roses to put in
here a slide, and there a swing.

Diversion

I noticed it day one and then forgot
the redbrick viaduct

till the Council boys
in the luminous hardhats and vests

raised scaffolding that cast shadows
straight and precise

as a map of the colonies
across the footpath and the green margin

where they've stacked the new sleepers
and earthed the transformer.

Damage

The tree that fell
into the road
the other day
has been carted
pathside overnight
and chopped in eight

The storm did it
but each goldhearted
lumber cylinder
is wormed through
like an apple
where an insect's hatched

Thank God she says
my nervous neighbour
that nothing worse . . .
a car crash . . .
think of how much . . .
what might have been . . .

The Street

Lee's car has sat on blocks at least six weeks.
He rolls off the tarp and we stand around his yard.
His friend Amit, he reckons it's the sparks.
Then Mr Kumar shuffles by, leaning on his stick,
with a can of petrol. He feeds it into his *Bluebird*,
straightens up and says, 'Nice day. Will get hotter.'
The rubbish is beginning to stink. The Council's on strike.
Kids suddenly mill around, chasing after
one another, and then they're gone again.
We mind our own business, no one says anything.
Mr Kumar enters his front garden,
gone a bit to seed, and the lawn needs mowing.
We pretend we are all looking at Lee's defunct car,
me, Lee, Amit, even David whose window clicks
open across the street. It's melting; is it the sun
that's stopped moving, or us? Mr Kumar darkens the front door,
faces up to its fish-eye lens, fingers his useless key
and presses the bell. The street goes quiet and sounds empty.
It seems to wait a minute, as if something
is about to repeat itself, even though there's no sign yet
of that door snapping open, of Mrs Kumar
with a stick or a rolled-up paper to fold and switch the air
around her husband's bowed and balding head, no sign
of his noise that goes nowhere but will fetch the large white van
and a policewoman, no sign either of how we'll start again
to speak to Mr Kumar about the weather, or the state of the road
and the chances of driving it in his *Bluebird* or Lee's *Colt*.

The Ice Carrier

He's in a little shiny tux, catching his breath,
leaning in a doorway and about to cart
into the freezing Cardiff night a basin of ice.
The street's mental with skinheads in T-shirts, tats,
and girls wearing Santa hats and bits of sateen.
Condensation seems to whiten his moustache.
He stiffens his back and braces his forearms,
zigzags across, an earplugged stray
out of tune with the street and its nightlife
which melts a path before his cloudy breath,
then sucks it shut as he quits the blasting cold
for the Pleasure Palace and its Happy Hour.

The Quarry

after Ronsard, and for Barty Begley

Just like a deer for whom the April sun
breaks the frosty morning's idle glaze,
who anticipates the new grass
and abandons the wood for the lure of the dawn,

travelling alone far from pack and crowd,
on bare mountain and grassy acre,
by lawless corrie, stream and river,
liberty her pole star, her pace unhurried,

her freedom unconscious and fearless,
till she's found, that is, by death's harness,
and murder's hand is dyed red in her blood:

like her, I knew routine without appetite
till a glance revealed the labyrinth and its exit,
stealing my fate for its own good end.

Day Job

The routine
is so entrenched and second nature
that a deviation like last night's party
which ended with your missing the night bus
and walking miles home in the snow
throws you right off

and you're still
so dustily numb and dazed from its after-effects
you can hardly tell if the day's grind has happened
or you are still walking home in the snow
wondering how on earth
you'll get through tomorrow.

The Electric Jar

Knowing its occult property,
its charge of static electricity,
a scholar in Leiden,
trying out new instruments, not a theory,
had air blown

into a dome of amber
from which he ran a damp wire
through a gun barrel
to a jar of water,
tapping a charge so reliable

it drew a crowd
which, for an open-air experiment,
held the wire and formed a circuit.
The idea, the instrument,
gripped and tethered

the curious and obedient
like revealed truth
or the shockproof future
that belongs to whatever power
draws such subjects to it,

occupying both town hall
and city street —
even as it solves, for all,
the black hole
that flows around their feet.

The Break

The middle-aged builders in the sunshine
knock off early for lunch,
idle on the steps and bitch
about a friend of a friend's lottery win

and *Big Brother* on the television,
or they talk up tonight's fixture
and its effect, for better or worse,
on their hopes for the season

which reside in the awning
of lunch hour's half-hour forum,
a breather that must defer
to the long,

allowing look
of the machines which launch
or re-launch, with shine and whirl
of cog and wheel and crank,

the workaday overkill
of grinding revs, and recall
the hired hands
to the mixer and the drill.

The Middle Kingdom: A Directory

For Receptions, Occasions and Venues, see the University, the Contact, Urmston Masonic Hall. 'Bowl a maiden over at the Lancashire County Cricket Club.' See Wedding Services. See Food. See Photos and Videos. See Clothes and Appearance. See Transport. See Religious Organizations.

For Religious Organizations, see also Churches, Church Halls and Places of Worship. See Church Furnishings and Supplies.

For Church Furnishings, see Reclaimers and Architectural Antiques. See also, Builders' Merchants, Demolition, Roofing Materials, Salvage and Reclamation, Masons.

For Masons, see Monumental Masons, Memorial Stone Masons, Drystone Wallers and Sculptors.

For Sculptors, see Pop Empires and Bright Morning Star (Or widen search).

For Bright Morning Star, see also under Calligraphy.

For Calligraphy, see Books, Rare and Secondhand, Factory Shops and Villages (See also Further Education; See Universities). See also Shopping Centres. See Decorations.

For Decorations, see Costumes, see Fancy Dress, Theatrical Supplies, Uniforms and Staff Wear.

For Uniforms and Staff Wear, see also Marking and Other Identity Services, see Barcodes, see Rubber Stamps, see Security Services and Equipment.

For Security Services and Equipment, see also Intercom Systems. See Closed Circuit TV and VTR. See Hi-fi. See Gifts.

For Gifts, see Flowers, see Garden Centres (See Nurseries, see Decorations), see also China and Glass (Crystal). See Wedding Services. See also Places of Worship, Church Furnishings, Masons, Sculptors, Decorations, Flowers. See The Moon Under Water for England's Finest Venues and Occasions. See The Chorlton Conservative Club, see The Black Lion (No Reception).

The Feast Day of the Assumption

When I asked you what was meant by it
you explained how it rose, like dust,
and disappeared into that dull steel pan of sky
where whenever we'd squint up at it
we'd somehow make out ourselves alone.

Wildlife

1 FOX

Mock dog, she stands up,
legs braced, angled,
her short stare

letting on, a second,
that something exists
beyond her black eyes,

adjacent to this,
and easy to enter
as pushing a door,

but then she is low, gone,
nosing along
some complex trail,

secret but evident
as the culverted stream
through next door's yard.

2 BLACKBIRDS

Since the gloomy top-heavy conifers came down,
an afternoon's work for three travellers with saws,
we've had, for weeks, blackbird after blackbird
descend fluttering on the lawn,
missing their landing place
but making off with what's been left behind.

3 ZEBRA

The toll mounts and it's a strange sight.
We can hardly believe that it exists
or that we're paying for it.
Embarrassing to say, it makes two points:
the heat is often torture;
everything could be black and white.

4 THE WOLF

'Time is a river that sweeps me along but I am the river.'
   — Jorge Luis Borges, 'A New Refutation of Time'

The wolf was slinking around the house
fairly friendly even though it frightened
my brothers, the small one the most,
it must have been me who had it sleep
by the back door rather than shot,
even when encouraged to do so by herself.
She said did she have to do everything,
but I would not shoot the gun
pressed to my sleepy, wolf forehead.
I'll do it myself, said she.

Interview

I read an interview
      where she talked about
how the most important,
      the lode-star events
of her life to date
      had not been the sort
which an image
      or a storyline
might, on average,
      be said to define
but instead rested
      at the fringe
of what might have been
      in the . . .
and she broke off
      or I was called from the queue,
singled out, like anyone,
      for a treatment
to which I alone
      would be subject.

Interference

I step into it as it surrounds me,
a patch of earth so hemmed in by trees
the branches meet over my head.
Another person, like a curtain in a sick ward,
draws the little light into her interfering voice.
What she says is nothing new:
'It will all come out in the wash.'
A stout short woman, of high colour,
she must drink alone at night
with that same narrow look of desire.

Will she still be there — a secret keeper — afterwards?
She'd said, 'I'm keeping my eye on you.'
I thought I saw her at an uncle's funeral,
and that day we moved house. I like to hear
little or nothing about her.
All this time, too, I feel
the damp heat rising out of the earth,
the wind shaking down the trees.

Tinnitus

My father's tinnitus is like the hiss off a water cooler,
only louder. And it doesn't just stop like, say, a hand-dryer —
    the worst is
it comes and goes. Or you shine a light on it
and it looks permanent as the sea,

a tideless sea that won't go away. The masker
he's been prescribed is a tiny machine, an arc of white noise
that blacks out a lot
but can't absorb the interference totally

any more than you or I — taking the air,
stirring milk into coffee, daydreaming through the six
    o'clock news,
trying to sleep on a wet night —
can simply switch off what's always there, a particular
    memory

nagging away, the erosive splash off a little river
wearing away the road, say, on the Connor Pass,
a day out, through which he'd accelerate
in the flash, orange Capri.

Not Getting Caught

i.m. Charlie Chute

The weekends
would melt
into the week;

we'd gather
each afternoon
at the tennis courts,

ditching bikes,
conspiring over partners,
arguing line calls,

next-door neighbours
but shy,
walking home alone

for tea,
corned beef
and diluted orange,

then out for more
or, if everyone
was talking,

a chase
through back gardens,
knocking down

apples or trampling
hedges or
rose trees

that had been
years
in the making,

maybe a life's work
or last weekend's,
enough that

sometimes
an adult
would emerge

red-faced
shouting
parents' names

(then Nero
barrelling
slowly out

panting, drooly,
always in
on these *scenes*,

these experiments
in causation,
how

we didn't do that
because
we did do this)

and catch
the straggler
or most forward one

and sometimes
one would
get caught

not like that
but stuck
waiting it out

while the rest
of us,
nettle-stung,

red-marked
from whippy
branches,

clothes stuck
to us,
ran off.

The First Person

The first person I see, the porter, is absorbed
in reading some life story or other. Beyond the foyer
empty corridors branch, turn and disappear
like a maze-path in an English manor.
He directs us to where we'll spend this long weekend,
but this is not a hotel, we're not on holiday,
and we're neither lost nor here by appointment.

It was three unsteady miles door to door;
we hit each bump and ramp from there to here.
'It's halfway over,' you said; I fill the car-park meter
and shoulder the suitcase and rucksack you'd packed,
and repacked, weeks before the due date crawled past.
We walk through clusters of smokers
who look frozen by a breath of fresh air,

past that bright desk and maze,
up stairs to the ward. Huge windows
admit daylight to a pristine landing we enter
and exit: there's not a soul in the corridor
till two nurses, gowned and sterile, hurry away
and others emerge at the duty station
to introduce the midwife by name

and confine us to Suite 5. It gets late
and nothing goes on, slowly, except pain
and its sporadic relief. The room's machine-lined
and half-lit and a simple bassinet awaits
the baby's red, shivering, world-shifting delivery.
He lies one night, blue-eyed, in the sleepless society
of other mothers and nameless neonates.

We bundle him into the morning,
mill through Wood Street and a lifting mist
so early that we startle birds, a building

of rooks, into the free air, and arrive home,
time-lagged, wakeful, tuned newly to what
scatters the quiet life's ticking clock,
shelves 'to-do' lists, and muffles with his slow

and yawning stillness the week-day world.

By Accident

The night our boy fell I was running late.
I made the unanswered call
under the city's bright,
then cloudy, skull
and, as the needle knows the north,

trembled at the shock ahead,
a house blacked-out and silent,
a night that, commuted,
ran to earth in accident,
a shorted circuit, you and he locked

into the diagnostic dark
in Park Royal intensive care
where consequences arc
beyond 'contusion', 'fracture',
the ward's humming network

to a different city, a year later,
the kind of night, calm, almost tranquil,
when he calls and haggles with his sister
even as we find more and more unreal
our imaginings, which were terrible.

Shouting Match

1 DADDY-LONG-LEGS

I'm upstairs when I hear a sound grow
into screams and laughter:
his hilarity is caused not by the spider
but by his sister's terror.

His wincing 'Oh no', though,
is caused not by the spider
or my heavy step on the stair
but his sister's low, harmless blow.

I might as well be the dangling spider
when I intervene between brother and sister
who grab my legs, eye one another
and shout themselves hollow.

2 SHOWER

Over the gush of the shower
I make out
the howling duet
in the corridor.

She has sat on her brother's old toy,
the 'really useful engine',
and her cry
is more of a crowing

which he takes in hand
by drowning her out
with a shout
almost as loud as my own.

3 SPORT

What I cannot hear
as the ball crosses the line
on the bar's big screen
to a gale of beery cheering
is the voice I use
on Sunday afternoons,
the voice of Law,
as I chastise

my children
when they ask
for coke then milk then water
while I try to concentrate
as the radio commentator
reaches one climax after another.

4 THE YARD

The yard can no more be split in two
than the house it backs onto
or is backed onto by.
In one corner a small, red-cheeked boy
looks through the fence's eye-sized hole
as if his yard is no more the whole
of the wide world
than the ball his red-haired sister has whirled
over the washing line
which acts today as a dividing line
across the muddy, green, uneven ground
and gives him grounds
to turn his back
even as his sister calls him back

to where, as things get out of hand,
the ball will land
on still-disputed land.

Clouds

Where I sit — in the uncovered stand,
beside me my copy of Han Shan —
might as well be the east face of Cold Mountain:
the rain rolls in, in waves. But let's stop
looking at the clouds. The ball's about to hop,
one man moves his feet fierce and quick:
the crowd, too late and almost to itself, shouts 'Pull'.

Beyond the posts, the planes, their vapour trails
lost in the clouds. Myself, I puck the odd ball
in back garden and public park,
once in a retired stadium, the grass knee-high,
vague and excessive as a cloudy sky.
A baby's crying ceases. It's a good connection.
Away it sails.

Japan

The weather is coming down around them and filling up the
    fields
but they are Sunday drivers, stuck in a dead end, with their
    heads
buried all the while in table-sized road maps that approximate
to where they live, in what we'll call the Hall of the Present
    Life,
its walls loud and impermeable as radio and its roof screwed
    shut
so they rarely notice the emissaries of the Hall of the Western
    Paradise
who dwell among them at crossroads, in courtyards and
    country lanes,
who take many guises, whose form is fluid and inconstant,
who will receive the souls of the dying believers,
who on their vests wear the names of those who paid for their
    creation,
who carry in one hand a rope for binding, and in the other
    a knife.

The Reconstruction

And in caved the ceiling's once-white render so the room was
    taller
as well as wider but what was hidden by the plaster

was four wasps' nests, two of them broken so the combs
showed, layered like a cross section of skin with black flumes

shot through; the others were streaked brown and grey eggs
from which they now curled like smoke or flags

unfurling even as the hired man, claw hammer in hand, froze,
facing something, in the dust, that settled and rose.

Title Search

Easy to establish that its plot is complex,
this building with its tiered, long-abandoned garden,
the broken frame of a one-time glasshouse
and the house itself really a balcony,
good for hot evenings with its view of the sea,
its red cracked roof a stop for company
who walk the cloud road to the old town
or do a little night gardening under the new moon,
miles anyway from the site of the old Registry
whose deeds occasionally reappear like fossils
to confound the titles we've pieced together
from translations, cheap shots and hearsay.

The Low Road

I turned back
and took the ferny, lower fork,
a return that veered towards a river sound
which itself seemed wound at a steeper arc
down to some deeper, blacker sound.

A deer backed clear,
its scut like a child's upturned nose,
and sprang away from the grass road
into a flurry of higher grass
up the pass

to the town's environs;
I should have followed, higher in the valley,
closer to the sky,
far from the anxiety
of that drifting moraine

of leaves and dusty pine cones
which felt as if it would give way,
the year's mossy detritus
a locally made
subsidized softness,

the tall and fallen trees
fording what might have been the river
not even a mile
from a knot of houses,
almost a village . . . But that was later:

first the sky would disappear,
the ground flatten to a cliff, bare and awkward
as a shadow on a small black river,
the same river that, as long as I walked,
I would not see but only hear.

'The Omen'

I crouch behind the sofa and scream
and my sister and girl cousin join in.
This is worse than any bad dream.
In the kitchen at the end of the hall
my mother and aunts must be cooking
or, when that's finished, even talking
about something important to us all.
When I go in all I see is smoking.

At the crack of dawn my father and uncles
had arranged themselves into a single car.
By the time they return from Clonmacnoise
we'll honestly say we almost made out
their voices in the enormous shout
that RTE will repeatedly televise.

The Quiet Life

Is it this you wanted, the still centre
of the quiet life, its ticking clock,
the white goods' hum and on/off click,
next-door's pipes and creaking stair?
It could be, let's face it, anywhere,
the usual birds sleep in its shadow
and from every side, in stereo,
a surf of noise going who knows where,
traffic clutching, flown, a landing plane,
the trains' two-beat come and go . . .
And outside the mirrored window,
closer to home, in the tended garden
and the undergrowth, what rustles
there, or in its wake, might be
grass stirring or, on *their* way,
even your discarded half-read papers.

You Interrupt

Purr and whistle, a change of gears,
the milk float, next-door's shift *and* the chorus
of robin, tit and blackbird: all have read
our waking up. 'Nearly 5,' you said,
'and it's already bright.' The children stirred,
but didn't wake: things could be worse.
Real coffee for an early start. The word
for this is long-lost, beyond use: it'll be years,
and what harm, before it gets a chance.
You interrupt, 'It's not like this:
it's the same as before'; birdsong, the steaming kettle . . .
Upstairs first one, then the other begins to call.
Is this enough? Will that be alright?
You'll go in a while; the traffic's still light.

Swallows

If it is true, and it *is* true, that winter
will strip bare

the perfect leafy trees, leaning them into one another
so the wires against their trunks

look like the sort of shape
where, in dreams, more than one will disappear,

it will leave behind
this ragged see-through bundle,

a bony hand, a metal frame,
an aerial

for what's not here, for that African chattering
above an empty field,

the evening drawing in
as you veer into view and call me on

along paths that twist and turn and branch
and never end.

Look

Do what you will,
the black cat
is perched on the sill,
same as last night
and the night before that.
You're away from us still.

**** **** **** *5443*

I'm held in the second bar
of the Revenue's *Casio* solo,
the hot receiver at my ear,
drumming the stairs with my free hand,
on my lap a sheaf of credit card statements,
like a book of lyrics,
each with a number and date, some named:
The Lime Tree, The Bookshop, Dove Cottage.
Dove Cottage: it's like I'm miles away,
not many moons ago, escaping a traffic jam,
walking up that dusty, cobbled sidestreet,
a dwarf orchard at one corner,
music too, from an open doorway,
money in my pocket, time on my hands.

A Minute

The Fog Lane short cut is barred by a tree chipper,
an army of legless conifers, and a trail of tinsel
and broken ornaments. The sky turns copper
and I start to remember how the rain would pour
at New Year's meetings in Limerick and Tramore.
But before the downpour, before I throw in the towel,
before I fumble, in two minds, for the mobile
and directions, I've a minute to consider
the roads Sunday-quiet, the bagels as yet unbought,
and how this day's carry-on seems now customary
as the new eruvs of Temple Fortune where, on Shabbat,
train lines and back-alleys host activity
undreamt of by the old Law on whose holy day
the baby should cry and cry, the meal burn dry,
speech disappear and even news of this stay put.

The Landing

I live for the wrong turns —
        a conversation about Canada
or Labour veering into
        how no one'd rather
be invisible than fly;
        the names of the trees
that shadow the walk home
        go missing among
Hollywoods and statins, then
        who'll pick up the children,
and where will we live?

        The past's a decrepit hotel: knock it,
we should inherit nothing . . .
        Maybe, you say, Hereford
and environs
        resemble nowhere more
than Waterford,
        the sort of dark place
where nothing has ever,
        ever happened:
I know this place well,
        working slowly backwards

to what I expect
        and least anticipate.

The Wake

Usually I haven't a clue, and would say so, but then
in the sort of place where you might most expect it,
a formerly grand hotel on the coast,
at a time, slightly between seasons, when the sea
hasn't made up its mind and in the morning
seems to divide mildly in two, dark and deep, then light and
     shallow,
so that the boats leaving port seem too quickly afloat
in the foggy, horizonal, sky-coloured tide

it is there and then I pick up not the thing itself but its trail:
from someone who seems as if he might know, a reflex;
from another, the story of a heartfelt response,
and for a while, a minute or two, or even a week, I think,
I gather, that what they talk about must exist.
It's just been hard to find and impossible to recognize.

Return

What looked like an omen was instead repetition:
I'd almost forgotten all about you.

The heat had put ants on the footpath
and, I checked, in the yard and kitchen:
the colony, true to form, had sent out
its little cartoon sentries and assembly line.

A nightmare. Even as I spray the place white
with *Ant-X-Foam* they scurry along the cracks,
burrow into the walls and flags and loam,
going off in all directions, scattered and clueless

like my thoughts when you enter them
in one of your many cameos,
crucifier, storm warning and the storm itself.

Someone, anyone, come.
Knock the walls, kango the floor.

Town

We leave tomorrow and the night finds me — where else —
down by the river, its current quiet and regular as a pulse,
silvery dark where the banked trees grow around
the outflow pipes. A bird takes off and goes to ground
in a commuter's site whose unpainted cement
is either half-finished or half-dismantled.
Farther off I see, bright as an oil rig, the Co-op shine
and foam, humming its bottom line.

The town's lit up, but no one comes back to reminisce,
intent as some evangelist smashing fossils,
making a religion out of feeling homesick . . .
Empty river, indifferent night: no joke.
We'll leave, grow older, return, say, 'Then what?'
On it all the glowing river twists the ground shut.

Hedge

I THE ONION HARVEST

You face me from one end
of the long waist-high hedge
like a train driver looking down
the barrel of his engine

but bare-chested, on holiday,
captaining this green train
that you've draped
with strings of onions

each green-brown, testicular bulb
like a light socketed from the earth
shining its spot or ball light
out of the glistening hedge

into the fir screen's grey-blue shadow
and your own grey, brown torso.

2 ROAD SAFETY

I check the convex mirror in the hedge across the way
and see, beyond plantations of fir and rowan,
the roadside monument to the killings
of 1918 and 1921
and, up the road, away from this house on its bed
of unravelled blue pencil and its hill of water,
the empty crossroads for Knocknagoshel and Duagh,
but from the hedge that frames this convex mirror,
wild with blackberries, gooseberries,
dribbling mice, a hen pheasant will soon wander
the grassy margin, among the thistles
and the ragwort and the nettles,
and will halt there a while, quiet out,
seeing time pass, looking in every direction.

The Hundred Towns

'There is no capital of the world.'
　　　　　　— Czeslaw Milosz, 'Bypassing Rue Descartes'

We negotiate
　　　　ring road, tunnel and ferry
　　　　　　but by noon GMT

are nowhere, ie, an endless suburb
　　　　stacked and balanced
　　　　　　like washing-up.

The day out seems set to fray
　　　　into a relief map of noise,
　　　　　　the kids crying *where*

until you call a halt
　　　　and we abandon the car
　　　　　　and follow a sign pointing east:

we reach the beaten path, tar and mud,
　　　　and trundle buggies up blind, rising corners,
　　　　　　piggyback past tourists consulting an A-Z

and a man with children who smiles
　　　　at the sight of us:
　　　　　　'another day in paradise . . .'

In a mile, an hour, we lay out the picnic,
　　　　a tartan rug on the side of a hill,
　　　　　　greenly adrift in the public park:

a barbecue smokes the wind,
　　　　a lean-to of a caff
　　　　　　hosts wake-up karaoke, blues and big band

(someone murders 'It's oh so quiet'),
    quad bikes buzz and weave
        earning a crowd with their figures of eight

and across the river Canary Wharf glitters,
    a sky-high shower curtain
        in the rainless weather.

Quick clouds flit in the sky's corners.
    Flat out in the heat like a film,
        the city's empty, the future of a hundred towns.

The kids run off; we share a cold and fizzy beer,
    but I close my eyes as you say, 'We could not,
        would not be anywhere but here,'

and I sleep off this well-planned afternoon
    from which, not soon enough, we'll double back
        making out signposts for home

that don't, at this distance, as yet exist.

The End of the World

A desk, three chairs, some paper,
paper clips, two elastic bands, a hole puncher.
A mini stapler. A note to say
a computer is on its way.
A fold-up map of the city centre,
an instruction manual for a printer. No printer.
A phone, a bin. And in the bin there's
a black plastic strip that bears
the name and title of the previous occupant.
A feeling that nothing will happen
if I don't pick up when my number is called,
if I idle at the desk instead
looking at the tangle of strings
that might operate the blinds,
thinking about a pun, or a metaphor,
and how,
          as a matter of fact,
it's not the end of the world.

Acknowledgements

Acknowledgements are due to the editors of the following publications where many of these poems, or versions of them, have appeared: *Agenda, AGNI, All Saints No Sinners, An Sionnach, Best of Irish Poetry 2007* (Southword Editions, Munster Literature Centre), *Cimarron Review, Éire-Ireland, The Irish Times, Magma, The North, Oxford Poetry, PN Review, Poetry Daily, Poetry Ireland Review, Poetry London, Smith's Knoll, Southword,* the *Times Literary Supplement* and *west47*.

An early version of 'The First Person' was originally commissioned by Matthew Caley as a response to Philip Larkin's 'The Hospital' and was exhibited as part of 'How Dish Wing' (*High Windows*) at the Poetry Café in London.